The symbolism of the shoe with special reference to Jewish sources

Nacht, Jacob

BIBLIOLIFE

REPRINTED FROM THE JEWISH QUARTERLY REVIEW
NEW SERIES
VOLUME VI, NUMBER 1

THE SYMBOLISM OF THE SHOE WITH SPECIAL REFERENCE TO JEWISH SOURCES

BY

JACOB NACHT

1915

THE SYMBOLISM OF THE SHOE
WITH SPECIAL REFERENCE
TO JEWISH SOURCES

BY

JACOB NACHT

TO MY CHILDREN

JEHUDIT AND DEBORA

THE SYMBOLISM OF THE SHOE WITH SPECIAL REFERENCE TO JEWISH SOURCES

EVEN the shoe has its history, its significance. Many a custom in connexion with the shoe which we practise blindly to this very day becomes of interest to the student of the history of civilization so soon as we set out to trace it to its beginnings. Then much that was unintelligible becomes clear, and new light is thrown upon many a popular custom. The following is intended as a modest contribution on the subject of the symbolism of the shoe.

Our first source of information concerning the shoe is the Bible. Here the shoe partakes of the character of the profane, symbolizing the Earthly in contrast with the Holy. Removing the shoes signifies putting off something profane, obligatory upon those who approach the Holy. ‘Put off thy shoes from off thy feet, for the place whereon thou standest is holy ground’, is the command to Moses (Exod. 3. 5). The Levites, whose function it was to carry the vessels of the Tabernacle, were required to take off their shoes while performing this holy service.[1] The priests likewise had to be barefooted when performing their service in the sanctuary,[2] this regulation has in part continued to be observed to this very day on the occasion of the Priestly

[1] Num. r. sect. 5 : במה היה יכבנו יל לוי מעולה׳ יישראל היו מהלכים לבויים כנדלים, אבל יכבנו יל לוי יהיו טעונים בכלי המיבן היו יחפים. הרי למדנו יהי׳ יכבנו יל לוי מעולה מכל היבטים

[2] Exod r. sect 2 : ובן הבהנים לא יבייו במקדיט אלא יחפים.

Blessing pronounced on festivals. As a matter of reverence,
no one with his shoes on should set foot upon the hill in
Jerusalem whereon the temple had stood in bygone days.[3]
This explains the custom current in some localities until
the late middle ages, that no one was to enter the synagogue
with shoes on.[4]   Only with bare feet should one draw near
to a place dedicated to God.[5]

   The shoe denotes supreme power and possession. ' Den
Pantoffel schwingen ' is a well-known proverbial expression
marking off the shoe as the symbol of power.   And another
adage, in which likewise the shoe is represented as the
embodiment of power, says : ' As long as thy foot is shod
tread the thorn.'   The shoe thus is accorded an importance
equalling that of the foot.   The foot signifies domination :
' Thou madest him to have dominion over the works of thy
hands ; thou hast put all things under his feet ' (Ps. 8. 6).
Hence the victor puts his foot on the vanquished to sym-
bolize the victory which has been won : ' Put your feet
upon the necks of these kings ' (Josh. 10. 24) was the order
of Joshua to his victorious warriors in order to indicate that
the enemy had been defeated for all time to come.[6]   And

[3] Comp. Berakot 54 a ; Yebamot 6 b ; RMbM., *Bet ha-Beḥira* 7. 12.

[4] עין או"ת מה"רם מינין ס' ל"ח „ומהאי טעמא (הגזכר בברכות דף
נ"ד וביבמות דף ו') יש ארצות שאין מתפללים רק יחפים בלי מנעלים.
וכרני כשהייתי פה בק"ק במבערג בימי חורפי שהי' תקנה ע"פ גדולים
שלא ישא' סנדלים לב"ה." ועין נידמן, התורה והחיים, III, צד 78.

[5] Ex. r. II, 13 : „כל מקום שהשכינה נגלית אסור בנעילת הסנדל"

[6] Joshua 10. 24-5   ויקרא יהושע אל כל איש ישראל ויאמר אל קציני
אנשי המלחמה ההלכוא אתו קרבו שימו את רגליכם על צוארי המלכים
האלה ויקרבו וישימו את רגליהם על צואריהם. ויאמר אליהם יהושע אל
תיראו ואל תחתו חזקו ואמצו כי ככה יעשה יהוה לכל אויביכם אשר
אתם נלחמים אותם.

just as the foot symbolizes power, so also does its gear, the shoe. Of the hero Joab King David says : 'And put the blood of war upon his girdle that was about his loins, and in his shoes that were on his feet.'[7]

The shoe thus characterizes the successful warrior. But it also denotes victory in a different battle, the battle for right and possession. A purchase becomes legal when the seller takes off his shoe and hands it over to the buyer. This ceremony indicates the transfer of possession to the new possessor. The same holds true of the redemption of property by one's kinsman, and also of transactions of barter 'This was the manner in former time in Israel concerning redeeming and concerning changing, for to confirm all things : a man plucked off his shoe, and gave it to his neighbour : and this was a testimony in Israel.'[8]

With the ancient Teutons likewise removing the shoe meant the transfer of power and symbolized the dissolution of property and inheritance.[9]

According to a haggadic narrative Mordecai established his right of dominion over Haman by producing a shoe on which was found a written statement by Haman to the effect that he had sold himself as a slave to Mordecai.[10]

[7] 1 Kings 2 5 · וגם אתה ידעת את אשר עשה לי יואב בן צרויה אשר עשה
עשה ליושבי שרי צבאות ישראל לאבנר בן נר ולעמישא בן יתר ויהרגם · · ·
ויתן דמי מלחמה בחגורתו אשר במתניו ובנעלו אשר ברגליו . Comp also
Schlesinger, *Geschichte des Symbols*, p. 235   · The removal of girdle and shoes is a symbol of conditional and unconditional surrender.'

[8] Ruth 4 7 : וזאת לפנים בישראל על הגאולה ועל התמורה לקים כל
דבר שלף איש נעלו ונתן לרעהו וזאת התעודה בישראל . Comp. also b Kiddushin 60 a.

[9] Grimm, *Deutsche Rechtsaltert.*, p 156

[10] Ag. Est ed Buber, V. 60   "מיד כתב המן על כנדל מרדכי : אני
הכן האנני עבדו של מרדכי היהוד' שנמכרתי לו בככר להם אחת.

In a well-known case the shoe is removed from a person in order to indicate that he has lost his authority over a member of his family. When a man dies without issue, his wife takes off the shoe from the foot of her husband's brother,[11] showing that henceforth he shall have no claim upon his sister-in-law's hand. The man without a shoe is the symbol of him that is incapacitated for marriage, while the shoe, on the other hand, marks off the aspirant to marriage.[12]

The shoe means possession in a larger sense: offspring, land. Moses lacked two things, land and children who would walk in his footsteps, hence the command to him is: Take off thy shoes (in the plural); but Joshua, though childless, entered the land, hence it is said of him: Take off thy shoe (in the singular).[13]

To loosen a person's shoe-strings, to carry his shoes after him, as the carrying of garments[14] in general, is equivalent to subjugation. The master gains authority

וכשעלה לבסוף לגדולה וקבע את עצמו את עבודה זרה והי' מרדכי יושב בשער המלך שהוא יוצא ובא בו וכשיהושוא ראה את המן שעובר הוא פושט לו את רגלו בסנדל שיטטר לקיחתו כתוב בו והי' המן רואה ומתמלא חמה".

[11] Comp. Deut. 25. 9.

[12] Comp b. Kiddushin 49 a : מסני דרב מכרעאי לא בעינא.

[13] Comp. Midrash, *Sekel Tob*, to Exod. : לפי שמשה רבנו לא זכה לישני„ דברים לא לכניסת הארץ ולא לבנים עומדים על מדרגתו, לכך נאמר בו של נעליך לשון רבים דהיינו שני נעלים . אבל יהושע נאמר בו של נעלך בלשון יחיד לפי שזכה לכנס לארץ אבל לא זכה לבנים עומדים על מדרגתו". See further מדרש חסרות ויתרות, ed. Wertheim, p. 50 · ואמר במשה של נעליך ונאמר ביהושע של נעלך לפי שלא נכנם משה לא"י ולא ירשו בניו מקומו.

[14] See b Erubin 27 b : מובילנא מאני'.

over his servant as soon as the latter loosens his shoe-string.[15]

To cast the shoe at a person is a sign of disrespect. The strong commit this act against the weak. 'Over Edom will I cast out my shoe' (Ps. 60. 10) God is made to say by the Psalmist. Like the glove[16] in later times, and the shoe of the league among the peasants,[17] so also transmitting the shoe serves as a challenge to fight and as a token of subjugation. 'Powerful kings in ancient times used to send their shoes to their inferiors as a sign of subjection. The shoe had to be carried on the shoulder as a mark of humility.'[18]

In the language of the Bible and the prophets the term shoe-string or shoe is also employed to express something petty and of little value. Abraham, who refuses to accept the least thing from the King of Sodom, says: 'I have lift up my hand (to swear) . . . that I will not take from a thread even to a shoelatchet, and that I will not take any thing that is thine' (Gen. 14. 23).[18a] Samuel likewise, in defending his honesty as a judge, protests that he had taken neither silver . . . nor shoes.[19]

---

[15] Comp. b. Kiddushin 22 b : כיצד בחזקה התיר לו מנעלו.

[16] Comp Nork, *Realworterbuch*, s. v. Schuh.

[17] 'The peasants employed the tied shoe, the union shoe, as a symbol of revolt', Schlesinger, *l. c*, p. 236.

[18] Grimm, *Deutsche Rechtsaltert.*, p. 156.

[18a] Gen 14 23 : אם מחוט ועד שרוך נעל. The poet Moses Dar'i (9th cent) likewise says of the insignificant price of the pen שרוך נעל מחירו בין צרכים לקוטי קדמוניות (Pinsker, צ"ז p, צ"ז).

[19] In accordance with Ben Sira of the Septuagint 46. 19 where Samuel is made to say. χρήματα καὶ ἕας ὑποδημάτων ἀπὸ πάσης σαρκὸς οὐκ εἴληφα. On the other hand, the greedy prophet has sandals and entrails presented to him · 'Whoever comes first as an interpreter of my verses, to him give new sandals . . . and fill his hand with entrails' (Aristophanes, *The Birds*, ll. 972-5).

To sell a person for shoes means to abandon him for a mere nothing, to tread upon him, as it were, with the shoe. When the prophet Amos reproves the judges in Israel who sell the poor for shoes,[20] he means to say in the first place that they wrest the judgement of the poor for a small bribe, but at the same time he wishes to emphasize symbolically that the poor is trodden upon 'like the dust of the earth'. The shoe which the corrupt judge receives is the symbol therefor. As men tread with the shoe upon the dust of the earth, so they (the unjust judges) desire to tread upon the head of the poor.[21]

The shoe as a symbol of somebody being trodden is found also among the Rapajutes in the following case: 'The Rapajutes let the criminal ride on a donkey through the city with a wreath of sandals around his neck.'[22]

In disputes the term shoe designates an insult in the highest degree. Thus the Arab women, in their mutual quarrels and altercations, call to one another: سرمتي على راسك, 'My shoe upon thy head'.[23] This derogatory exclamation characterizes the authority of the one over the

---

The Indian teacher, after the distribution of the Samāvartana sacrament, receives shoes as an honorarium (Glaser, 'Der Indische Student', *ZDMG*, LXVI, 28).

[20] Amos 2. 7 : עַל מִכְרָם בַּכֶּסֶף צַדִּיק וְאֶבְיוֹן בַּעֲבוּר נְעָלִים. Comp. also Yalkut to וַיֵּשֶׁב and פִּרְקֵי דר״א : וַיֵּשֶׁב and וַיֵּשֶׁב at יִשְׁמְעֵאלִים בַּעֲשָׂרִים at יִשְׁמְעֵאלִים בַּעֲשָׂרִים to Yalkut כֶּסֶף כָּל אֶחָד וְאֶחָד מֵהֶם נָטַל שְׁנֵי כְּסָפִים לִקְנוֹת מִנְעָלִים לְרַגְלֵיהֶם שֶׁנ׳ עַל מִכְרָם בַּכֶּסֶף צַדִּיק וְאֶבְיוֹן בַּעֲבוּר נְעָלִים. Note also the piyyut in allusion to this agada : (מוֹסָף לְיוֹ״כ) אֵלֶּה אֶזְכְּרָה in the piyyut לְאוֹרְחוֹת יִשְׁמְעֵאלִים סְחָרוּהוּ בְּעַד נְעָלִים נְתָנוּהוּ.

[21] *Ibid.*, 2. 8 : הַשּׁוֹאֲפִים עַל עֲפַר אֶרֶץ בְּרֹאשׁ דַּלִּים.

[22] Comp. Nork, *s. v* Schuh

[23] Similarly, Gen. 3. 15 : הוּא יְשׁוּפְךָ רֹאשׁ וְאַתָּה תְּשׁוּפֶנּוּ עָקֵב.

other, who is to come under her shoe. To come under the shoe or to lick somebody's shoe exemplifies slavish subjection,[24] while handing a shoe to a person should be construed more in the sense of devotion. Thus the son hands the shoes to his father, and similarly the pupil to his teacher.[25] The custom among the Sarmatae to toast the beloved by drinking from her shoe is likewise to be construed as an act of homage.[25a]

The dependence of the son upon the father and of the pupil upon his teacher is expressed by the formula that the father or teacher strikes the son or pupil with the shoe.[26] Conversely, a woman who threatens to strike her husband with the shoe wants to emphasize her authority and independence.[27] In certain cases the woman has a right to hit

[24] Esther r. 8. כי מי אני אשר לא אשתחוה להמן על תשועת עמך
ישראל, כי לוחך היתי מנעל רגליו. In striking resemblance is the custom to kiss the slipper of the Pope. In the same connexion I wish to call attention to a passage in Aristophanes (*The Acharnians*, ll. 300-1), where the enemy is threatened with being cut up into shoe-soles 'For I hate thee still more than Cleon, whom I will cut up into shoe-soles for the Knights'

[25] p Shabbat VI, 1 (p 8 a) : שמעון בר בא הוה מישמש קומיה ר' יוחנן ר' יוחנן והוה מוישיט ליה סנדליה.

[25a] Comp. also Goethe, *Wahlverwandtschaften*, p. 258 (ed. Kurz, vol VI) ' Ein schöner Fuss ist eine grosse Gabe der Natur . Noch immer möchte man ihren Schuh kussen und die zwar etwas barbarische, aber doch tiefgefühlte Ehrenbezeigung der Sarmaten wiederholen, die sich nichts besseres gönnen, als aus dem Schuh einer geliebten und verehrten Person ihre Gesundheit zu trinken '

[26] Comp b. Moed Katon, p 25 a נפח ליה אביה בסנדליה. Similarly, Nork, s v. Schuh 'Not until the end of his term of apprenticeship is the Brahman pupil permitted to wear shoes, for these are signs of independence' Comp also Glaser, 'Der Indische Student', *ZDMG*, LXVI, 25 'He (the Indian student) should not approach him (the teacher) with his shoes on '

[27] Aristophanes, *Lys* 658 τῷδέ γ' ἀψήκτῳ πατάξω τῷ κοθόρνῳ τὴν γνάθον.

B 3

her husband with a shoe. In a portion of Russia it is
customary for a woman who is insulted and called indecent
to strike her shoe in the face of her insulter.

As a symbol of contempt for one and esteem for the
other the terms sandal, shoe-latchet, shoe-sole, and shoe
generally, are employed by both Arabs and Jews in certain
turns of speech. The Arab Bedouin, when separating from
his wife, says: 'I have thrown away my slipper.'[28] The
eastern Jew often expresses his appreciation in the following
words · 'He (resp. you, &c.) is not worthy to loosen his
shoe-strings,[29] he has more sense in his shoe-soles than
you in your head ;[30] he is as wise as my shoe-sole.'[31]

A woman scorns a Rabbi by telling him that her father's
shoe was worthier than his entire family.[32] In Palestine
the word shoe or shoemaker serves as a disgrace. When
somebody mentions 'shoemaker' in his conversation it is
always with the addition: Far be it (this handiwork) from
you. Never is the word used in a favourable sense. It is
considered a great dishonour to be dubbed 'shoe'.[33]

---

[28] Nork, s. v. Schuh

[29] Comp. besides Luke 3 16 ἔρχεται δὲ ὁ ἰσχυρότερός μου, οὗ οὐκ εἰμὶ ἱκανὸς λῦσαι τὸν ἱμάντα τῶν ὑποδημάτων αὐτοῦ

[30] Literally עֶר האט מעהר שֵׂכל אין דער פידעזשוע וויא די אים קאפ.

[31] Literally: עֶר אין קלִיג וויא מִין פידעזשוע. Comp. also the Rumanian popular expression: 'vita incaltata' (a shod animal), which resembles the Hebrew בהמה בצורת אדם applied to simpletons

[32] עין „לקט הקמח" ביֹֹֹֹֹֹֹשם הרי"טין: „החכם שנדה את האישה וכ' על ייזלזלה אותו ונגעה בכבודו, העזה פניה ותאמיר לו שהמנעל של אביה הי' חישוב יותר מכל משפחתו"

[33] See Luncz, לוח א"י, p. 47 : המנעל ועושהו נחשבים אצל אזרחי הארץ למושנים של גנאי, עד כי בהזכירם את השם סנדלר, הם מוסיפים דרך כבוד: בַעיד מִנַֿך, לאמר רחוק ממך או לא עליך. ולעולם

Fine feathers make fine birds' is a proverb frequently
cited, while Homer says: 'Through handsome garments
one obtains favourable repute among the people.'[34] In
Biblical literature, to mention but one example, we find
a similar attitude in the exhortation: 'Let thy garments
be always white.'[35] In the Talmud, besides clothes in
general which, according to Ben Sira, illustrate the worthi-
ness of man,[36] special emphasis is laid on foot-gear. In
the shoe the value of man finds its expression.[37] 'Only he
who has shoes is a man.' The slave goes barefoot. One
should sell everything in order to obtain shoes,[38] for he
who walks barefooted is placed in ban by God.[39]

When putting on shoes a certain blessing is required.[40]
There is likewise a definite prescription for the manner in
which to put on or take off the shoes. In putting on shoes
the right foot has the precedence, while in taking them off
the left foot comes first.[41] Especially important is the foot-
gear of women. Moral motives were responsible for these
sayings. While it is said of the vestments of women in

לא יעלו את היטם נעל על דל שפתם עם איזה מושנ של יבח, ולעלבון
גדול יחיב לאיש בהקראו ביטם נעל.

---

[34] Comp. Homer, *Odyssey* vi, ll. 29-30:

'Εκ γάρ τοι τούτων φάτις ἀνθρώπους ἀναβαίνει
ἐσθλή.

[35] Eccles. 9. 9 : בכל עת יהיו בגדיך לבנים.

[36] Comp. ענג יבת (Frankfurt a. M., 1700) where it is cited in the name
of Midrash Tanḥuma : וכן בן סירא אומר הדר אלקים בני אדם והדר בני
אדם כסותו See Zunz, *Gottesdienstliche Vortrage*, p. 104.

[37] Comp. b. Shabbat 122 : מנעליה ברגליה בר אניש.

[38] b. Shabbat 129 a : לעולם יביור אדם קורות ביתו ויקנה מנעלים
לרגליו.

[39] b. Pesaḥim 113 b.

[40] b. Berakot 60 b.

[41] b. Shabbat 61 a, and *Derek. Erc*, ch. 10.

general : 'With her dress a woman removes also her
decorum ',[42] the Rabbis went even farther in considering
as a transgression the baring of only certain parts of the
body. Attention should therefore be paid to the foot-gear
of women, especially those living in cities. Thus, while the
man in the country was permitted (on the basis of an oath)
to forbid his wife the wearing of shoes for a period of three
months, this prohibition was valid only for twenty-four
hours in the case of a city resident.[43]

As a whole the woman enjoyed more liberties than man
with respect to foot-gear. Thus the male had the same
shoes for week-days and sabbaths,[44] for father and child ; [45]
furthermore, he is to wear a pair of shoes seven years.[46]
Not so the female, who was at liberty to obtain a pair of
shoes for each of the three holidays.[47] These regulations,
as indicated above, were dictated by moral motives. Hence
the song of the royal bard on the feet of Zion's daughters :
'How beautiful are thy feet with shoes' (Cant. 7. 1), provokes
the censure of the Haggadist : ' Such eulogies are not fit
even for an ordinary man.' [48]

Nevertheless attention was paid to the aesthetic needs
of women with regard to the cover of the foot. Apart from

[42] Herodotus, I, 1. 17.

[43] p. Ketubbot, VII, 31 b : בכפרים יכול הבעל להדיר את אשתו שלא
תנעול מנעל עד ג' חדשים, אבל בכרכים רק מעת לעת.

[44] p. Shabbat, VI, 8 a לאו אורחי' דבר נשי' מחוי ליה תרין סנדלין
חד לחולא וחד לשובתא.

[45] b. Shabbat 112 a : רב סלא הוה ליה ההוא זוגא דסנדלי זמנין דנפיק
ביה איהו, זמנין דנפיק ביה ינוקיה.

[46] b. Giṭṭin 68 b : שמעיה לההוא גברא דהוה קאמר לאושכפא עביד לי
מסאני לשב שני.

[47] b. Ketubbot 65 b.

[48] Cant. r. 7 : אפילו הדיוט מקלס בלשון זה גנאי הוא לו.

the shoes common to both men and women, which, be it
remembered, were not without gold ornaments, there was
already at the time of the Talmud a distinct fashion for
feminine shoes [49]

As in the case of women, there are also special prescriptions for the foot-gear of scholars. While, on the whole,
a person wearing shoes that have been patched is equal to
the barefooted, this is especially true of the learned. It is
unworthy of a scholar to walk the street with patched
shoes.[50]

The scholars who used to mourn for Jerusalem, known
by the name אבלי ירושלים[51] and distinguished through their
exterior apparel, also wore shoes of a black colour.
As a token of mourning the shoes as well as the latchet
were black.[52] Only the worthiest could make use of this
foot-wear. Unknown people were forbidden to wear such
shoes, and when they were found doing so were subject to
punishment.[53]

As a rule shoes were black, latchets white. This was

---

[49] b. Shabbat 141 b: לא תצא אישה במנעל המרופט, on which comp.
Hirschberg, *Ileatid*, IV, 51: והתקישטו במנעלים איזר יש יהיו נם מוזהבים
והיו מישותפות בהם עם הנברים · · · אולם כבר נמצא נם מנעל מיוחד
לנשים · · · סנדל האישה היו מזרבים במוך.

[50] b. Ber. 43 b: גנאי לת"ח שיצא במנעלים המטולאים ביוק.

[51] Comp. J. Klausner in *Ilaomer*, II, 9

[52] Tosafot Baba kamma 59 b, *s. v.* הוה ורמם': ומסאני אוכמי דהבא
תענית היינו המנעל והרצועות הכל הו' שחור.

[53] b. Baba kamma 59 a-b: · · · אליעזר זעירא הוה מרים מסאני אובמא
איטבחוהו דבי ריש נלותא וא"ל מאי יניא הני מסאני? א"ל דקא מאבילנא
אירושלים. א"ל את חשיבת לאתהבולי אירושלים? סבור יהורא הוה
אתיוה והביטוה.

the Jewish custom.[54]   In order to escape the persecutions
of non-Jews,[55] it was permitted to wear also black latchets,[56]
'so as not to be recognized as Jews'.   On the other hand,
if a Jew is requested 'openly' to wear his shoe-latchets in
accordance with non-Jewish fashion, he must under no
conditions yield to this request.[57]

Another phase of the shoe which deserves attention is
the interchange of shoes in putting them on.   Thus the
doctors of the Talmud made it their practice on holidays
to put the right shoe on the left foot and the left shoe on
the right foot.[58]

Various symbolic effects are attached to the state of
being barefoot.   Fugitives and captives go without shoes.
King David removes his shoes as he flees before his son
Absalom.[59]   The prophet Isaiah is ordered by God to go
barefoot [60] as a symbol of the capture of Egypt and Cush
by Assyria.   'And the Lord said, Like as my servant
Isaiah hath walked naked and barefoot three years for
a sign and wonder upon Egypt and upon Ethiopia ; so

---

[54] See Tosafot, *l. c.* ואומר ר"ת דהמנעל הי' שחור והרצועות לבנות.
On the various kinds of shoes, comp. b. Yoma 78 a–b : תוספות ינעים, *s. v.*
בין לר' מאיר.

[55] b. Taanit 22 a : א"ל מה טעמא ראמית מסאני אוכמי ? א"ל עיילנא
ונפיקנא ביני עכו"ם כי היכי דלא לידעו דיהודאה אנא. As to change of
clothes in order to avoid danger, comp. Gen. r., sect. 82 : שינו עטיפתם
בשעת השמד.

[56] Tosafot, *l. c.* : ומסאני אוכמי דמס' תענית היינו המנעל והרצועות
הכל היה שחור.

[57] b. Sanhedrin 74 b.

[58] b. Taanit 12 b : מרימר ומר זוטרא מחלפי דימינא לשמאלא ודשמלא
לימינא.

[59] 2 Sam. 15. 30 : ודוד עולה ובוכה · · · והוא הולך יחף.

[60] Isa. 20. 2 : ונעלך תחלוץ מעל רגלך.

shall the king of Assyria lead away the Egyptians prisoners,
and the Ethiopians captives, young and old, naked and
barefoot.' [61]

The removal of shoes symbolizes, as already mentioned,
resignation and loss. At the decease of a near relative,
such as parents, children, or brothers and sisters, the wearing
of shoes is suspended for seven days. The same observance
holds true with reference to mourning in a wider sense
Thus on the ninth day of Ab, which is observed as a fast-
day in memory of the destruction of the Jewish state, it is
likewise forbidden to wear shoes. The same is also true of
the Day of Atonement, when Israel prays for forgiveness,
for life.

Every great disaster which befell the people was indicated by the removal of shoes. Dearth of rain caused the
sages of the Talmud to take off their shoes as a sign of
universal mourning [62] One doctor of the Talmud is famed
for having obtained the object of his prayer with only one
shoe off, when rain began to come down.[63]

The removal of shoes designating loss and suffering, it
becomes evident why the carrying off of shoes by the dead
appearing in dreams forebodes evil and disaster.[64] For the

---

[61] Isa 20 3-4 ויאמר יהוה כאשר הלך עבדי ישעיהו ערום ויחף שלש
ישנים אות ומופת על מצרים ועל כוש . כן ינהג מלך אשור את שבי
מצרים ואת גלות כוש נערים וזקנים ערום ויחף

[62] b. Taanit 24 b

[63] *Ibid.*. רב יהודה כי הוה שליף חד מסאנא אתי מיטרא   Owing to
a superstition it is forbidden among the Arabs to walk with only one
sandal : ' Do not walk with one sandal in the manner of the devil is one of
the commandments in the *Kitāb ākāmi' l-murgāni* (quoted from a review by
Nöldeke in *ZDMG* , LXIV, 444)

[64] b Berakot 54 b: כל דישקיל מעלי בר ממסאנא וכנדלא .   In
Germany a superstition prevails that a guest must not be presented with

same reason the retention of shoes after death is considered
by some people as a favourable symbol. This custom was
known already at the time of the Talmud,[65] and has been
preserved until this very day among the Jews of Tripoli.[66]
It was familiar also to the ancient Norsemen.[67]

Widespread is the custom of offering gifts to the bride.
The bridegroom gives presents to the bride. This custom
is rooted in antiquity: it probably dates from the time
when woman was still considered the personal property of
the husband. This state is expressed symbolically by the
present which the bride receives from the bridegroom,[68]
and is borne out especially by the circumstance that the
present consisted mostly and still consists of shoes. Such
was the use among the ancient Lacedaemonians,[69] and so,
as we shall see further on, it has been preserved among
other nations until this day. The shoe proclaims symbolically: The man is the ruler in his house. ' The govern-
ment of the house was assumed literally the moment the man
set his foot upon that of his bride ; the slipper furnished the
symbol for it '.[70]   In handing the shoe to the bride the

shoes lest he should depart soon and never return. (Fischer, ' Die Quitte ',
ZDMG., LXVIII, 298)

[65] p. Kilaim IX, 32 b : ר' יוחנן הוה מפקד אלבישוני חוורין ויהבין
מסאני ברגלי.   Comp. Krauss, קדמוניות התלמוד, I, 125, n. 2.

[66] Comp. אפריקה של היהודים בטריפולי in *Hamebaser*, Constantinople,
1910, p 204 : עוד מנהג במקום הזה : המת יקובר יחד עם כל הנעלים
שהיו שייכים לו.

[67] See Nork, *s v.* Schuh

[68] Comp Bebel, *Die Frau und der Sozialismus*, p 33 · 'Symbolic for the
acquisition of woman as property is also the present which the bridegroom
still offers to the bride in all the civilized countries.'

[69] Comp. S. Fl Marianu, *Nunta la Romani* (Hymeneal Customs among
the Rumanians), Bucharest, 1890, pp 258-9

[70] Schlesinger, *l c*, p. 331.

bridegroom considers himself as her conqueror   Mighty
kings sent their shoes to inferiors as a sign of subjection,[71]
while, according to an old German practice, the bride considers herself subject to the bridegroom the moment she
puts on the shoe which he gave her as a gift.[72]   Accordingly
the man is the shoe which the woman has to wear.

This symbolic designation for the man is not unknown
to the Talmud.   A woman, according to one passage,[73] may
annul a contracted marriage if it is found out that her
husband occupies a higher rank and station than the one
she believed him in originally.   She may say : ' I have no
use for a shoe that is too large for my foot.'

While the transmission of the shoe to the wife signalizes
the assumption of the rights of the husband, the man who
allows himself to be dominated by his wife is stigmatized
by the nickname · man of the slipper ', that is, not the wife
but the husband wears the shoes which should be worn by
her as a token of his power.   He is the subjected party.
As a Yiddish adage has it   ' Az dus weib geht im spodek,
geht der mann in pantofel.' [74]

As a rule, therefore, the woman must wear the slipper
or shoe which her husband has bestowed upon her.   The
shoe must be neither too small nor too large for the
foot.   As mentioned above, the woman may say of her
unevenly contracted marriage : · I have no use for a shoe
that is too large for my foot '.[75] while, on the other hand.

[71] Grimm, *l. c*, p 156.   [72] Grimm, *l. c* , Nork, *s. v* Schuh.

[73] b Kiddushin 49 a   מכאנא דרב מיברעי לא בעינא   Comp hereon
Horace, *Epistulae* 1 10 42 ·

   Cui non conveniet sua res, ut calceus olim,
   Si pede maior erit, subvertet.

[74] Comp. Bernstein *Judische Volkssprichworter*, p 88.

[75] See above note 75

Aschenputtel becomes the bride of the king's son after it is found out that the golden slipper presented to her by the prince fits her foot. The fitting shoe decides the right choice.

> Rucku di guck! Rucku di guck!
> Kein Blut in Schuck.
> Der Schuck ist nicht zu klein,
> Die richtige Braut, die fuhrt er heim.[76]

Among a portion of the Palestinian Jews it is customary to make sure of the fitting of the bride's shoes, and for that purpose the bridegroom sends the cobbler to his bride's house. Simultaneously with this ceremony the day of the wedding is determined upon.[77]

In general, however, little importance is attached to the fitting of the shoe. The main thing is that the bride, and also her relatives, are presented with shoes. That also the relatives of the bride are presented is probably due to that ancient custom according to which the kin of the bride should appear in the same dress as the bride herself. Thus among the ancient Greeks the bridemaids had to be dressed in exactly the same manner as the bride. Says Athene to Nausicaa :

> Nausicaa, has thy mother then brought forth
> A careless housewife? Thy magnificent robes
> Lie still neglected, though thy marriage day
> Is near, when thou art to array thyself

---

[76] Grimm's *Marchen*, Aschenputtel.

[77] Luncz, כשבועים לפני החתונה שולח החתן p. 12 ,לוח א״י, תרס״ט
לבית הכלה רצען לתפור לה מנעלים כדי מדתה וזה סימן כי זמן
החתונה הוקבע.

In seemly garments, and bestow the like
On those who lead thee to the bridal rite.[78]

It is a practice among the Sephardic Jews that the bridegroom, before the wedding, bestows shoes upon the bride
and certain members of her family.[79] The handing over of
shoes to the bride immediately before the wedding is related
by Gregory of Tours.[80] In Teheran the bridegroom, soon
after his engagement, sends shoes to the bride, her mother,
and her sisters.[81]

The Russian peasants employ the boot as a symbol in
choosing a bride. As soon as the son makes known his
preference for a girl, the father, on a Sunday, orders his son
to bring his two boots, one after the other. In one of them
he had placed (some time previously) a handful of oats.
'If the son brings this one first, it is a sign that the alliance
will be successful and blessed. If, however, the son seizes
the empty one of the prophetic boots, fate wills it that the
chosen girl cannot be his.'[82]

Among the Rumanians[83] the bridegroom transmits

---

[78] *Odyssey* vi, ll. 25 9.

Ναυσικάα, τί νύ σ' ὧδε μεθήμονα γείνατο μήτηρ;
εἵματα μέν τοι κεῖται ἀκηδέα σιγαλόεντα,
σοὶ δὲ γάμος σχεδόν ἐστιν, ἵνα χρὴ καλὰ μὲν αὐτὴν
ἕννυσθαι, τὰ δὲ τοῖσι παρασχεῖν οἵ κέ σ' ἄγωνται.

[79] See הספרדים מהיי by אלמלוח in *Hashiloah*, XXIV, 267 . לעת ערב
לפני החתונה יׂולח ההתן לארוסתו נעלים ולכל המׂישפחה.

[80] Comp. his *Vitae Patrum*, ch XX, cited by S. Fl. Marianu in his *Nunta la Romani*, pp. 58–9.

[81] *Revue des Écoles de l'Alliance Isr.*, for 1901, p. 166. 'Le jeune homme envoie aussitot à sa fiancée, à la mère et à chacune des sœurs de celle-ci une paire de souliers'; comp. also M. Grunwald, *Mitteilungen*, &c., XX (1906\), 132.

[82] 'Russische Sitte' in Wolfgang Menzel's *Morgenblatt* for 1838, p 635

[83] Marianu, *Nunta la Romani*, p. 239: 'Mirele cumpera si pereche de

shoes to the bride and to her mother, or, when the latter is not alive, to her representative ; while among the Bulgars the bridegroom has to bestow shoes upon all the members of the bride's family.[84]   In many localities of Italy slippers are sent instead of shoes.[85]

Finally, mention must be made of the custom current among English-speaking nations to throw slippers after a newly-married couple departing for their honeymoon. This custom is in vogue even among the highest circles of society,[86] which, however, did not deter an American mayor from prohibiting further exercise of the practice.[87]

This prohibition calls to mind a similar decree issued in 1690 especially against the Jews of Hesse.   Here, too, it was customary for the bridegroom to bestow slippers upon the bride and her family on the day of the wedding.   The Hessian diet considered this an extravagance not permitted to the Jews, which should be opposed as extravagance in dress generally.   The diet therefore issued an order that the gifts should be limited to the bride only, and should consist only of a pair of shoes and slippers.   This custom has been preserved up to the present among the Jews in

papuci san crobote pentru . . . mama miresei, car daca mama acesteia nu traeste, apoi pentru cea ce o suplineste.'

[84] 'Volks- und Familienleben in Bulgarien', *Sarajevoer Tagblatt* for Aug. 15, 1913

[85] Comp. Marianu, *l. c.*

[86] *Neue Freie Presse* for July 9, 1913 (No. 17556)· '. . . Thus the family of the whilom English Consul-General Crave preserves a ball shoe of white silk and with gold embroidery, which the Prussian crown-princess, later Empress Frederick, removed from her foot in order to throw it into the carriage of her court maid, who had just been married to Joseph Crave.'

[87] *Ibid.*: 'In Portsmouth, Ohio, the mayor and the chief of police issued an edict, according to which the police are authorized to arrest every person who strikes newly-wed people on the back, or hurls rice upon them,, or throws old shoes after them '

Hesse, where the bridegroom, on the wedding day, gives to the bride a pair of shoes as ' סבלונות '.[88]

The shoe is also the symbol of courting and fertility. Among the English-speaking nations[89] rice and slippers are thrown after the betrothed couple as a sign of fertility, while, according to a Jewish-mystic interpretation, the biblical phrase . ' Take off thy shoes ' (in the plural) designates Moses, who was the father of two sons.[90]

In order to attract man, the women of antiquity used to expose their ankles[91] while Greek women employed the shoe as a means of embellishment. If a woman was of small stature she padded the shoe with cork in order to appear taller ; if, on the contrary, she was too tall she put on flat shoes.[92] Clemens Alexandrinus relates likewise ' that by means of characters imprinted in the sandals they indicated by footprint a rendezvous to their lovers '.[93] The Haggadah also mentions this practice. In commenting on Isa. 3. 16 Rabbi Jose remarks. ' The picture of a serpent was impressed upon the shoe ; the Rabbis however, have

[88] Comp Munk, ' Die Judenlandtage in Hessen-Cassel ', *Monatsschrift für die Wissenschaft des Jud.*, XLI, 520.

[89] See above, note 87

[90] Comp. מישה שקים פ"ו נאמר בו יול נעליך . מישה v s , ילקוט חדש.

[91] Comp *Healid*, IV, 52, n 1 ; also Herodotus, I, 395 . ' The women of the *Gidans*) wear many leather bands around their ankles, for the following reason, it is said . Every time a man knows her she attaches a band around her ankle.'

[92] Comp *Healid*, IV, 50, where Hirschberg points out a parallel passage in Lev. r sect 16. הלוך וטפוף תלכנה וברגלים תעכסנה . בישהיתה אחת מהן ארוכה היתה מביאה שתי קצרות ומהלכת ביניהן, כדי שתה' נראית יבה, ובישהיתה אחת מהן קצרה היתה לובישה קורדקין עבין ומביאה שתי קצרות ומהלבת ביניהן, כדי שתה' נראית ארובה.

[93] Comp Nork. s. v Schuh.

this to tell : The wanton daughters of Zion used to place in the heels of their shoes the stomach of a cock filled with odoriferous oil ; and whenever a host of youths passed by, they pressed their foot on the sweet-scented oil, so that the odour produced confusion among the youths like the venom of serpents.' [94]

As a symbol of love we also find ' the flowered shoe of the bat ' in the Chinese folk-song : ' Bat, bat, with flowered shoes, accompany us—the little girl yonder will be the wife, and I the husband.' [95]

The bride herself, as a rule, puts on the shoe given to her as a gift. Yet in the poem of King Rother the suitor orders one gold and one silver shoe to be forged, and he dresses the bride's feet which lie in his lap.[96]   In Berry the bride used to stand barefooted before entering the church for the wedding. The relatives endeavoured in vain to have her put her shoe on, since this could only be done by the bridegroom.[97]

In general, as already mentioned,[98] the putting on and removal of the shoes has to proceed according to definite

[94] Lam. r., IV : ובנרגלים תעכסנה, ר' יוסי אומר שהיתה צרה צורת דרקון על מנעלה ורבנן אמרי שהיתה מביאה זפק של תרנגול וממלא אותו אפרסמון ונותנה אותה בין עקבה למנעלים וכשהיתה רואה כת של בחורים היתה דופקת עליו והי' אותו הריח מפעפע בהן כאותו ארס של עכנא.—As to the serpent being a symbol of fertility, comp. Rubin, *Agada u. Kabba a*, pp. 18-19, and on the cock, p. 23. Comp. also Koran, Sura 24.

[95] *La Revue*, March 1, 1913, p 98 'Chauve-souris, chauve-souris aux souliers fleuris, accompagnez-nous, la petite fille que voilà sera la mariée et je serai le mari.'

[96] Nork, *s.v.* Schuh.

[97] Marianu, *Nunta la Romani*, pp. 258-9 'In Berry miresa statea eu piciorele goale coud sosea timpul sa mearga la biserica si rudele si cercan in Zador sa o incalta. Numai mircle isbutea '

[98] Comp. above, p. 9

prescriptions. In this connexion many mystic conceptions grew up concerning the importance of the feet and shoes. Thus it is said of Enoch that he effected the union of the upper worlds and knew how to keep the evildoers from himself through being a shoemaker.[99] We find further in a mystic book that the feet need special protection against the pernicious influences from the outside (חצונים), since they (the feet) represent the 'lower wisdom'. This protection is afforded by the shoes just as the Tephillin indicate the light of the face. On account of this similarity between Tephillin and shoes the left shoe is to be fastened first.[100]

'Civilized people lose easily their religion, but rarely their superstitions', says Karl Goldmark somewhere. The superstition concerning the shoe has come down to our own days, and we meet it even among the educated classes of society. Says Dr. J. Kohler, professor in the University at Berlin. 'My superstition is prognostic throughout; I place much

---

[99] See ילקוט הדש, s. v. אלוה': מצוה בני ז' מצוה אלא הי' לא הנוך
נח והי' מתחלה חסיד מחסידי או"ה, אלא יבפריש מדרכיהם והלך בדרכי
יברא? במי יבאינו מצוה ועוביה או כעין גר צרק שבכל דור ודור ונתקבל
במעלה העליונה לאות ולמופה לבני יבת מה כהתוק להם אם יטיבו
דרביהם ובין שעלה יבוב לא ירד. והנה כביב למחגהו ריבעים יתהלכון
המבקשיים להפריד ה"ו והוא הי' הופר מנעלים לקיבר העולמות.

[100] לקוטי הלכות על י"ע א"ח לבעל לקוטי כהר"ן, צד ז': יצריך
לנעול יבל ימין החלה ולקיבור יבמא? ההלה ולמדו מתפלין · · · כי המנעלים
הם יבמירה לרגלין, כי ברגלין צריכין ליבמור ביותר מן ההצוגים הסביבים
אליהם. ר' הרגלים הם בה' חבמה התאה בה' תבלית הצמצומים יצריבים
להתהבם מהר' מלביות ולהעלותן לבה' אור הפנים יבבתליב רגלים. ומיבם
נמיבבין בה' המנעלים יבהם יבמרים את הרגלין מן הצוגים וזהו כתפלין
יבהם אור הפנים בידוע כך במנעלים, כי כיבם נמיבך בה' המנעלים יבהם
בה' היבמירה לרגלין וע"ב בקביבירה יבמיא? ההלה כמו התפלין.

weight upon the right or the left shoe being put on first, because I imagine that otherwise something uncanny would happen'; while Tilla Burieux, the actress, states in an interview that she is very careful not to place her shoes on the table, because it signifies 'certain stuttering'.[101]

Concerning the laying on of the left shoe the following belief prevails in Ansbach : · If the bride lets the bridegroom buckle on her left shoe, she will rule in the house.' [102]

With reference to worn shoes the Chinese say · ' He who wears his hat sideways, has a lazy wife ; and he who has worn shoes on, has a gluttonous wife.' [103]

Finally, mention must be made of the superstition prevailing among a considerable part of the French people, according to which the preservation of the bridal shoe guarantees a happy conjugal life.[104]

[101] *Berliner Tageblatt* for May 11, 1913 (No. 235).

[102] Nork, *s. v.* Schuh.

[103] J. Banzemont, ' Enfants Chinois ', *La Revue*, March 1, 1913, p 102 : ' Si vous portez votre chapeau sur le col vous avez une femme paresseuse, dit-on, si vous portez un habit crasseux et des souliers eculés vous avez une femme qui aime à manger '

[104] *Revue des Deux Mondes*, Jan. 1911, p 146 ' Garder les souliers avec lesquels on s'est marie, c'etait s'assurer des chances de faire bon menage.'

BIBLIOLIFE

Old Books Deserve a New Life
www.bibliolife.com

Did you know that you can get most of our titles in our trademark **EasyScript**™ print format? **EasyScript**™ provides readers with a larger than average typeface, for a reading experience that's easier on the eyes.

Did you know that we have an ever-growing collection of books in many languages?

Order online:
www.bibliolife.com/store

Or to exclusively browse our **EasyScript**™ collection:
www.bibliogrande.com

At BiblioLife, we aim to make knowledge more accessible by making thousands of titles available to you – quickly and affordably.

Contact us:
BiblioLife
PO Box 21206
Charleston, SC 29413

Lightning Source UK Ltd.
Milton Keynes UK
UKIC01n0134030114
223852UK00001B/2

* 9 7 8 1 1 1 3 3 0 6 9 6 8 *